The Last G

To Rachel,
best wishes,

Shirley Wright

[signature]

Indigo Dreams Publishing

First Edition: The Last Green Field
First published in Great Britain in 2013 by:
Indigo Dreams Publishing
24, Forest Houses
Cookworthy Moor
Halwill
Beaworthy
Devon
EX21 5UU

www.indigodreams.co.uk

ISBN 978-1-909357-32-7

British Library Cataloguing in Publication Data. A CIP record for this book can be obtained from the British Library.

Designed and typeset in Palatino Linotype by Indigo Dreams.
Cover design by Ronnie Goodyer at Indigo Dreams

Printed and bound in Great Britain by Imprint Academic, Exeter.
Papers used by Indigo Dreams are recyclable products made from wood grown in sustainable forests following the guidance of the Forest Stewardship Council.

For Jim and Caroline

Acknowledgements

Acknowledgements are due to editors of the following publications in which some of these poems (or versions of them) first appeared: Roundyhouse, The Sunday Telegraph, Equinox, The French Literary Review, Poetry Monthly International, The Ver Prize Anthology 2010, The Interpreter's House, Earthwords.

Longing is posted on http://andotherpoems.wordpress.com

My Father won the Sunday Telegraph/Rose Theatre Poetry for Performance competition – thanks to judges Ben Okri and Andrew Motion. *Skin* was highly commended for the Ver Prize. *When She Died* was highly-commended in the Torbay Open Poetry competition.

CONTENTS

The Last Green Field

But at my back I always hear
Time's winged chariot hurrying near.

Andrew Marvell
"To his Coy Mistress"

And thine too is the last green field
That Lucy's eyes surveyed.

William Wordsworth
"I travelled among unknown men"

"The historical sense involves a perception, not only of the
pastness of the past, but of its presence."

TS Eliot

Climate Change

There are polar bears in my kitchen.
Environmentalists can stop worrying about
loss of habitat, population decline;
round here conversation maintains a steady sub-zero
and the icebox extends way beyond the fridge.
Arctic winds shiver the cornflakes and
I am wall-eyed, blinded by snow,
though frostbitten fingertips recall
when flesh flung hosannas
from your coat-hanger shoulders,
my rolling hips, when roaring kisses, raging lips
lit fires enough to burn the sky and scorch the sun.
This white-out rondo wounds our dream-thin skin;
ice cracks the toughest rock.

Femme d'un certain âge

"Looking the worse for wear," said the face in the mirror
without bothering to ask my opinion.

"You're only as old as you feel," said Grandad
tweaking my skirt and pinching my bum.

"Don't be such a baby," said the nurse
hefting a hypodermic harpoon.

"Interfering old cow," said number-one son
cursing my concern in metaphor.

"Won't you ever grow up?" said hubby
 threatening to trade me for a sleek-suited sophisticate.

"Smooth those wrinkles away," said the glossy advert
dicing with botulism.

"Can't stop worrying. You're still my little girl," said Mum
frantic over the telephone.

"Check-ups for the older woman," said the mass-produced letter
from the breast-cancer clinic.

"Life begins at forty," said a birthday card
negating four decades.

"Love you," said my lover, loving me, lovingly.

I went back to the face in the mirror
and stared for a long time;
then, breathing hard,
obliterated it entirely.

Skin

Nîmes, one slow September afternoon,
late heat bruising the soles of my feet,
the sun hanging whiter than the moon;

in dazed thrall, I drag you down the street
to ogle the shop window. The bag,
dead centre, pouts like lipstick – complete

redness, the wet-look, *like a red rag
to a bull*, you say, laughing at me,
at my desire blazoned like a flag.

Fingertips paddle my spine as we
kiss, our lips slick with sweat, think we hear
the crowds roar, think our half-closed eyes see

the curve of the Arena, smell fear …
To the café opposite to drink
Pernod, breathe Gucci. Atoms cohere

in the scent of leather, in the chink
of ice on glass. Calmly we discuss
dinner to coax the day into sync:

there is steak saignant, salade verte, plus
the bag on the table between us.

Cross My Heart

We ought to have a little chat:
a heart-to-heart, face-to-face,
tête-à-tête, spade-a-spade,
what-you-will,
heartfelt, hard-nosed, full-on
gut-spill.

I'm sick of mincing words,
this half-hearted tip-toeing round
on eggshells;
we need to break a few,
smash through,
tell it like it is,
make an omelette.

And while we're mixing
culinary metaphors,
it's a tough old muscle,
the heart;
rustle up some sage and onion,
gas mark four (at most)
a long, slow roast,
still needs chewing,
gravy to wash it down.

So mine won't break –
heart of oak, nerves of steel,
though people say I'm
too soft-hearted
for my own good,
say I wear my heart on my sleeve,
that I haven't the heart
to rip yours out,
not heartless enough
when it comes to the heart of the matter.

I always thought home was
where the heart is,
where you hang your hat,
keep your cat,
hearth and home –
one letter more or less
makes a difference,

Actaeon, changed to a hart,
ripped apart by his own dogs
for offending Artemis.
Think on that
and get back to me.

Getting On

If there's one thing that really
pisses me off,
it's that absent-minded whistle
hiss you do
through your front teeth,
irritating and off-key,
and the way you bristle
if I dare to criticise
or even wince.

While we're on the subject,
just empty the dishwasher
instead of moaning
there's no clean cups,
like that's a defect
in my character.
And buy your own biscuits
if you don't like custard creams.

Next time we're lost
try asking someone
for directions; I'm sick
of going round in circles –
another of my imperfections,
no doubt, like
preferring conversation
to football, like

being scared of
dying and not knowing
how to handle the going,
the how and when
and where, and you saying
you don't care
(in that annoyingly calm voice)
not to worry,
you'll be there.

My Father

loved fish – their slither
and slide, the rainbow flash
of scales that would leap
and glide past
in silence.

He raised me in his fishing basket
next to pike and tench
flip-flopping their tails
in my face, their scent in my nose
like earth and freezing rivers.

In the half-dark
we'd say nothing for hours,
our mouths
a wide O of astonishment
at the noisy world.

I ate fish bait for tea, played
with worms; fish hooks held
my nappy fast. Father
smoked beside the tide,
its rise and fall like my breath.

All summer we lay there,
the fish and I, beneath
latticed sunlight,
our round eyes staring;
we waited for him to take us out,

throw us back,
anything.

November Observance

When she makes a wish her lips move, paying
homage. She washes each currant by hand;
pours brandy liberally, conveying

heady transcendence; stirs the mix and
smiles as if blessed or blessing. Spices
fill the air, buttery prayers expand

into rich fruit cake that she will ice
with swirls of impossibly white snow;
then pop a Santa on top. Once, twice

she pirouettes for puddings, then throws
coins in for luck. Adds almonds, glacé
cherries, and Muscovado that flows

like wickedness – she's still a sassy
broad, my mum, a lady on whose face
time rests easy, bearing that cachet

of common sense folding into grace.
Knuckles like burst stars brush hair away
as she winks, *your turn*. I take my place

in the dance, acolyte here to say
the secret words six weeks early. Spoon
poised, I ladle generous holiday

hope onto whispered fears, *I'm sorrys*, croon
hallelujahs for the three of us,
the magical mystical triune,

her, me, and a Christmas pud.

Growing Pains

I grew up in a greenhouse
competing with the stink of tomato plants
whose fat fruits would split
then burst, from forcing.
My sweat slicked cucumbers,
dripped onto lush lettuce leaves
crinkled with organic vigour.

Father was a thorough man,
much taken with seed catalogues
and the value of fertiliser.
He practiced how to sow,
prick out and pot
only the strongest plants
(the weak just so much rubbish
for the compost heap) –
row upon row of cabbages,
marrows the size of Mozambique.

Mulched regularly
I flourished through the seasons;
friable soil around my feet
ensured deep-rooted dreams.
In winter fug, condensation
trickled down those endless
panes of glass like tears;
come sticky heat
my pores were clogged
with acne and John Innes No 3.
Me and Early Perfection peas,
ripe for the picking.

One day when spreading dung
and liquid manure,
and permanganate of potash,
and standing knee-deep
in rich organic muck,
I dared to ask him
about university –
he believed in hothousing.

London Pride

Sunday roast tastes of
Forces' Favourites,
coal dust on the hearth,
bakelite ashtrays spilling fag-ends,
ration books,
powdered egg;
and every swallow's
a crack in the lino,
and Anaglypta
rips my throat.

I step right through
a shadow of liberty bodice
fastened tight with rubber buttons
that crush my ribs;
and here I am
late for school again
wading the pea-souper,
breathing mouthfuls of
wet scarf.

I run so fast
I trip and fall over
past participles; yesterday lying
showered in flowers that
burst the pavements
cracked by bells which
rang from Bow to Haggerston,
where pearly kings sang
and trolleybuses clanged
the air.

Monday morning
I'm wrestling tights
and a sudden seam snakes my leg
like an eel
slithering thigh-high,
jellied, perhaps, with pie and mash
and pease pudding. And in the house
a ghost is whistling
Maybe it's because I'm a Londoner,
and I just
        can't
           breathe.

London Pride is a saxifrage that grows aggressively and thrives in urban spaces; its masses of pink flowers colonised bomb sites after the Blitz and came to symbolise the resilience of Londoners.

Breakfast

She calls it cooked food – fried eggs,
underdone, that slosh across my plate
like white-water hazard.
The snapped command not to wait.
Eat, or else. Keep the cold out –
a many-headed monster about
the house; Hydra
in slippers, stockings worming round her spindly legs,

a fluffy dressing gown. Other days
stuff like Vesuvius erupts
up my nose, down
my throat where porridge lava crusts
my heart. *Leave that, you'll get what for.*
Keep the cold out. Or coat the floor
in sick. Her knack, her art –
entombing fault in rock, her contrary sculptor's ways,

or witch, soothsayer, Gorgon,
winding me up to pips on the BBC.
I swallow against the clock.
Buck your ideas up, or see
what happens to naughty girls. Keep the cold
out. Out? I'm shivering now, not bold
enough to answer back,
cringing. What happens next's a foregone

conclusion. Bundled in a scarf,
I'm posted through the front door onto
icy pavements,
off to school on wobbling blue
legs warmed to red by her ready hand,
stamped with her special lasting maternal brand,
its pattern burning;
it'll keep the cold out. Be my epitaph.

Rough Magic
(en route to the Bath Literature Festival, Feb 2009)

Jammed between pink thighs and froufrou frills,
beneath the mannequin's snooty stare –
a bust of the Bard
roughcast in white plaster with
Hell's empty, all the devils Я here
scrawled in black felt-tip across the chest.

Nose pressed to the boutique window
I study the message,
observe how the pen has slipped,
pressed harder here, wobbled, left
an inkblot nestled in the hollow –
a mole unknown to Elizabethan scholars.

A label dangles from his chalky hair:
the dress-price cut, reduced, then slashed again,
brazen in shop lights that splash
the pavement, spilling onto clipped festival feet
that hurry to spend an hour in the company of
"one of our most important and popular novelists"

whose words can wrap the heart
in cashmere, organza, Balenciaga, and
on their sustaining garments not a blemish;
so reassuring in these tempest-tossed times
when coffee seems naughty at two pounds fifty
and hell is queueing for tickets to hear
a famous poet prattle.

I unstick my nose,
rub its cold tip,
smell wet glove,
city grime with low notes;
wander off
hoping for a glimpse of Prospero.

The Persistence Of Surrey

On his Sunbury sundeck
Mr Darly is busy painting.
He struggles with time
that slithers from his plate
like the ripe Camembert he ate
which oozed forth
lunch and inspiration.

Greasy fingers twiddle
imagined mustachios,
pick his nose, fiddle
brushstrokes in the booze-soaked
drowse of a suburban afternoon.
Indoors, cool in shadows,
daughter Jane practices piano,
playing Lenin on his skull.

Through the open window
comes the crash of Mrs Darly
slamming drawers,
each one a wreck of bones
upon a desert floor where desire
runs liquid and memories
are propped on flimsy crutches
scarcely strong enough to bear
the weight of longing.

He stares, bug-eyed,
as sand trickles through –
a temporal troubling of the medium,
his canvas like the landscape of his mind.
Clocks chime, ants scuttle,
Mr Darly plans supper –
a crayfish, perhaps, red wine,
then news on the BBC.

Conned Or Conniving?

Artists have conned us for years,
all that guff about fading beauty,
art defying the ravages of time –
just to get their leg over.

All that guff about fading beauty,
that *gather ye rosebuds* ploy
just to get their leg over –
what a bloody nerve.

That *gather ye rosebuds* ploy?
Bet some coy mistress fell for it.
What a bloody nerve,
exploiting fear to nail us.

Bet some coy mistress fell for it –
bludgeoned by an ego the size of Everest
exploiting fear to nail her,
she'd have mistaken lust for love.

Bludgeoned by an ego the size of Everest
it's impossible to resist
and easy to mistake lust for love.
A nip-'n-tuck only goes so far,

though it's impossible to resist.
Once wolf-whistles stop, we fake it,
but a nip-'n-tuck only goes so far
if our eternal summer's fading fast.

Once wolf-whistles stop, we fake it,
let art defy the ravages of time
if our eternal summer's fading fast.
Artists have conned us for years.

In Case You're Wondering About The Carbon Footprint

PC Grainger checked the photo,
reckoned it was loot from a bank heist
in Milan last summer.

The repairman remembered seeing
Made in China stamped
along the left-hand edge.

Lambeth Lenny tapped his nose:
"Fell off the back of a lorry, that did,
nudge, nudge, know what I mean?"

Our next-door neighbour, the ufologist,
swears it was snuck out of Area 51,
citing evidence of alien technology.

Mum thought it came
from *Toys R Us,* turn left
off the roundabout at Cribbs Causeway.

Jeff, impressed by gold tooling,
estimated Eighth Dynasty Egyptian
and muttered about tomb raiders.

The vicar said it was like love,
a gift straight from God,
on loan and not to own.

All I know is
I had it yesterday on the train
and now it's gone.

Painting Mrs Giocondo

He offers wine, heavy, red, for steady
nerves (his or hers?). *To warm you, Lisa.* She
hesitates, shuffles on the hard seat, sips.
Their fingers touch. He notes how her lips part
grape-stained, then close impassive as her gaze.
The brazier spits thin heat into draughts that
gust the room. She shivers, quick flicks a frown.
Try thinking about... Easy for him to
conjure vistas, passion, balls aching still
from slim boys behind Santa Croce. *Aah!*
escapes his throat. He lays her hands gently
one on the other, whispers in her ear
(his job today to humour and beguile)
lifts his brush, stands back, waits, to catch her smile.

Sky Speak

Few at first,
they swarm at dusk
when doubts come,
long shadows from the east
splashing the sky
like Rorschach blots.

As soon translate
Pushkin or Proust
as starling;
erect a scaffold of syntax
from which to hang
nouns, verbs,
then commas fly away

into dizzy air,
a murmuration
that swoops and falls,
furls on a thought
to rise and swoop again
as if in answer to some
wonderful calling voice.

The heart stops –
deep in folds
of our reptilian brain
there is a stirring
of words on the wing.

All The Time In The World

"J'ai appris très tard à aimer les oiseaux
je le regrette un peu"

    Au Hasard Des Oiseaux
    (Jacques Prévert)

Freedom and flutter,
the heavy beat of a woodpigeon
winging air, magpies
that strut my lawn,
the claw and beak
of it all.

Thrush song, a robin's nest,
sparrows monkish
in brown habits,
but ready to hustle
a plastic feeder
hanging from the sycamore.

They line the fence
in a pretence of manners,
hop and bob
before diving, mob-handed,
like feathered greed
poised on light.

We understand one another;
I keep my distance,
let them be. Avian high-jinks
recompense my slow morning coffee.
Regret's a jejune notion;
more importantly

patience, a willingness
to stillness,
to happening upon
the chance of birds,
the miraculous, unpredictable
moment of birds.

Morning Cuppa

Waves slosh up one side,
muddy-brown, very Bristol Channel;
reckless I jump in
nose-diving steam
to breathe the dreams of Assam
that lounge the Brahmaputra;

fronds in the amygdala uncurl,
soak up the moisture-rich
morning sauna,
a tropical rain shower
wanting only
the squawk of macaques
to complete the journey

from here to there.

Instead, the radio
huffs Humphrys,
an acerbic wheeze
that makes me splutter
tea across the kitchen,
wasting antioxidants;

my cupped hands
hug the heat exchanger,
grow human,
phalanges melt
in peaty acid tannin
and the hot heaven
of a caffeine ride
that buzzes brain back

from there to here.

Sabotage

Bluebells in a jamjar,
cool wind on hot summer nights,
a snatched throat-catch of Satchmo –
　　so brightness comes
　　rolling on waves that splash
　　the horizon at my feet.

In the thinning of the trees
the deer's eye holds my own,
slow-watching, patient –
　　we acknowledge one another
　　then move on,
　　blessed unexpectedly.

Autumn fruit falls,
Newtonian, prophetic, the grass
awash with jewels –
　　hedgerows hang heavy
　　bruised with the bounty
　　of garnet, amethyst.

Stick-of-rock sweetness
bears *yesterday* all the way through till
mouth melts with memory –
　　toes curl in wet sand,
　　the sea is in my ear,
　　and me standing here

sun-stunned
by moments,
fragments that stop the hourglass
　　like clogs hurled in the machine,
　　with all the fury and
　　astonishment of small things.

Biology Lesson

Aims
To be brave enough
instead of squeamish, girly;
to open a magic door and stare;
to win sixpence off my brother.
Thus I, aged eleven,
about to dissect an earthworm
dug up from the garden.
Not just me, of course, the whole class
after morning break, in double biology.

Materials
Mr Brice demonstrating
in lab coat and daps
with holes where his toes poke through
(he's a Morris dancer
and very into pigs' bladders).
A kidney dish clattering with
forceps, dissecting scissors,
special pins for skewering flesh to wood.
Sunshine through open windows,
the *thock* of tennis balls on cat gut.

Method
With conviction
make the first incision, then it's
precision and manipulation, observation
followed by tabulation, calculation and many
other words ending in I O N
without which there is nothing
but humiliation.

I lift delicate skin
and snip an opening in
for the scissors to
cut a line straight
(well, nearly)
from clitellum to mouth.
I ease the body apart,
clip through segments
(*segmentation supports diversified functions*)
pin back each tattered flap to reveal
shattered wonder.
I make notes in my new lab book
(left-side lined, right-side plain),
sketch diagrams, record
everything I do, everything I see,
draw arrows, label organs,
underline each one neatly
with a ruler.

Observations
The earthworm has five hearts.
Helen Fipps fainted because
Gareth Jones flicked bits of worm at her.
Worms are a fiddly undertaking
compared with rabbit parts
pickled in jars round the wall.
Outside, a crack when a car starts.

Conclusions
The worm was alive.
Now it's dead.
I killed it.
I'd rather do English.
(Underlined twice.)

Galahad

Can you grow roses on the moon,
catch the sky through the eye
of the storm, can you
find a unicorn and drink
its tears of longing?

These things are not impossible,
miracles still occur, you know;
after all, I met you
in the bus queue
that day the sun shone.

Are you handy with superglue,
can you repair what's broken,
sew up open wounds, fit
the jigsaw back together
when there's bits missing?

Knights of old would have had a go,
but they were bold, undaunted,
spangled with magic;
now it's Ikea and the flat
pack. Are you up for that?

Friday Night

Not even rush-hour jams enrage –
my car coasts the commuter crawl
light as air, its tyres dreaming
wide horizons, tea in bed,
a long lie-in Saturday morning.

Shoulders drop, unknot as
time eases through bone
and muscle; neurons fire;
Andromeda slides into view
above ranks of traffic lights
all bearing the same message.

Ahead of me, the elastic evening
gleams brighter than my TV screen,
brighter than my bathroom tiles
that wink agreement as I
bathe in bubbles, luxuriate,
exfoliate, moisturise, perfume,
apply face cream, preen.

There's no hurry. Clocks run
backwards and in the garden
worms turn sluggish, snails slow
to contemplate important things,
planets in their motion pause
and take a breath. Reminds me
of the sound my grandma used to make,
last thing, when she peeled her corsets off.

Her Voice

in the quiet house, a fall of
    words that
drift into the womb to float
    like plankton
waiting to bloom and feed
    small fish.

Around her the room
    settles itself
for talk of daffodils, the crib
    he painted,
chosen names, baby clothes in
    neutral shades

like morning light. Rocking to
    ocean tides
that pull her dreams, she croons
    Bob Dylan,
comfy in the wooden chair,
    heavy-breasted,

eager to explain how the cat
    knows, why
her dress no longer fits. The waiting's
    nearly done;
the Pacific plankton bloom is visible
    from space.

After Visiting *Dans Maen*

Here, my love, upon this beach
where foam-white water-whisper
spills across our narrow feet

I turn back to consider
other footprints, other tracks
worn into this ancient land.

Watch, and we may see them pass,
feel grass move, the heft of stone,
smell the rank sweat of purpose,

ache of bone. In cromlech,
cairn and maidens' dance they tread
still, though our faint steps are gone,

the sands washed clean. Shadows leap
against the seethe of evening –
listen! Can you hear them, breathing?

Dans Maen is Cornish for The Merry Maidens, a Neolithic stone circle near
Penzance.

Acton Court

She floats
on a hum of traffic
lapping her ground.
It is the latest circling
because the moat has long since gone,
dried to a child's pencil-line
that designates the house and garden
where metal pigs snuffle grass.

She sails
on waves of brickwork
so choppy I might be washed away
in the flood of years, but
am rescued by graffitied boats
and notes from scripture –
four-hundred-year-old *vox pop,*
dated but unsigned.
Banksy would love it,
that urge to speak your mind
then run away.
Plus ça change, as they say …

And yet I fear today will deluge history
in the slosh of fresh plaster,
new wood, a portaloo,
but mainly in our presence here;
we, the people, the common man,
come to gawp and wonder.
King Henry would never have believed it –
plebs peering at his privy.

How to navigate a course?
We cast off for Glastonbury,
Avalon, unsure
of what we may find.
They say there are ghosts,
if you listen.

Acton Court is a Tudor mansion in Latteridge, near Iron Acton, Bristol.

Field

It is a loss of air –
a slow breath which once expired
is gone for ever;
hear the echo of axe and falling
in that long, slow exhalation
of dying –
   field –
the place where trees are felled.

Today we move
through patchwork,
the vulnerability of fields
neatly crocheted at the edge
like blankets thrown across
some giant's rough-made bed
to smother Arden.

Only the mystery of wood,
the longing for it,
can sail time's ocean;
we trust to planks that creak
in the creep of dark places
but stay watertight, swell
with promise of shelter,
the forest floor.

Fields are emptiness
stripped bare of everything but field
until there's nowhere left to hide
our frailty, no tilt
of canopy or cooling shade,
no glade to lift hope
high enough for myths to sing

the branching of our story –
born in the heart of wildwood,
nurtured by wolves
and told in antique voices
to the trees that built us,
whose paper holds our dreams.

Fandango SW3

Orchids in the Jardin du Luxembourg
on show just one day a year – imagine!
Chelsea *week* seems excessive, gives the urge

to dance in Lady's Slippers, high-mountain
beauties whose pouch is foot-shaped, bee-burdened,
buzzing with perfumed hairs that lure me in

where tempo is tango, not Strauss; blazoned
frills twitch purple, flash glimpses of hot thigh,
fleshy folds that fill and spill abandoned

lust. A quick twirl, then it's ice cream. You sigh
as we lick vanilla, tra-la, tra-lee,
planning next year's borders. One can't deny

some folk feel faint, flower-dazzled, need tea;
thank God for Titchmarsh on the BBC.

On Chew Valley Lake

Sheet-still, metal-sheened,
the water throws me back my face,
sunlight glinting off my specs;
reflects behind my head
clouds, like woolly mammoths
grazing sky, nibbling air,
careless of the flooded fields beneath.

Trailing fingers disturb the mirror finish,
dabble drowned apple orchards,
paddle country lanes, lost plains
where fish swim in liquid reverie. I hear
farm carts creaking, the shriek
of kids at play, mill wheels grinding
the slow grit of grief down
years of human occupation.

The glass shivers,
as on the bank an ice-cream van
announces Ninety-Nines with chocolate flakes;
and in the lake the sunken village,
drowsing to the water's susurration,
dreams of summer heat and reparation:
tree stumps rising, hedgerows, Moreton bridge,
a young girl crossing the road.

South Of Sarum

Cars trundle, there and back again –
the A30 Cornwall to London
become a ribbon of memory
potholed with jellyfish,
oil slicks, plastic bottles,
silky sand beneath my toes
left over from yesterday,
a seaside gift still drifting.

Beyond the line of sky
the stones are waiting,
moon-swung megaliths
untainted by Factor 15
yet smooth to the touch.
Fingers on the steering wheel
fumble an echo of their song;
what's imprinted long in granite
has resonance – they are
yesterday's cathedrals,
not exactly Starbucks, but useful,
with a purpose.

At the service station I stop,
ignore the stench of petrol,
fill up with recollections
breathed deep; the tang of seaweed
and the salty sting of mornings
that sever there from here;
think "Nearly home"
even when I know otherwise.

Midnight On Harris

Sun sets slowly in the Hebrides, night
a half-forgotten tune that shivers memory
till it might just nudge a grudging shadow
across this June evening of warm winds and rose-pink light.

We scramble up the highest dune to watch
the display, see Taransay ignite. Clouds
like falcon wings sweep the sky bright carmine
where the sun sinks in a demonstration swatch

of colours my cheap camera cannot hope to hold.
I wonder where do vampires go, and old
old horrors; if the dark itself takes fright

and slinks away to howl the missing moon?
Stars struggle in a sky like afternoon,
the day unending, the wide beach flushed white.

Past Imperfect

In Beijing she bought pearls,
ropes of creamy white
so lustrous her neck
blushed with satisfaction.
He photographed the Imperial Palace,
its animal statuary –
lion, turtle, crane,
symbols of longevity.

In Shanghai she bought jade
earrings in softest green
quickly put to shade
by her dazzling emerald eyes.
He captured the sizzle of street food,
the drift of incense rising
behind saffron-robed monks
at prayer.

In Hong Kong she bought silk
underwear so fine a whisper
might bear it away,
and voluptuous bedding.
He used deep focus to record
boiling cocoons unwound
by hand in long, continuous strands
of gossamer, ready for spinning.

At home she shows off
their holiday snaps:
yet more roof tiles, flying eaves,
Ming tombs on the slopes of Huangtu,
a zigzag bridge, koi carp leaping,
rickshaws stuck in traffic,
another Buddhist temple.
Darling, where was this one?

The Gods Of Calanais

Patience must be one requirement – to stand motionless
for millennia, yoga-straight and soaring, with no
expectation of relief except where sky bursts
the eye of sunrise warm across three-billion-year-old gneiss,
throws light on saddle querns, arrowheads, artefacts
from a past held fast within their arms' wide circle.
Chiselled giants, they note the transit of Venus,
scratch their rough heads and make anthropological
observations about small creatures that crawl
through the miasma of peat-bogs, mist-monsters.
Tasked to watch the slow roll of a world
wind-whipped by the breath of history,
they count moon-landings, the illustrious dead,
endure.

Calanais is a stone circle on the Isle of Lewis, Outer Hebrides.

Then

Was it always summer,
frisbee on the beach beneath
skies that knew only blue
or pink or molten burning
at midnight?
Such visibility and glare,
a world too wide
for my hungry eyes
that would ache and stare.

Here at home
in an afternoon of heavy dark
and drawn curtains,
red coals instead of sun,
I sip tea grateful
for balance restored.
The day should turn,
and I am glad to feel its shudder,
like the slow closing of a door.

The Last Green Field

High up, about to float through the ceiling,
I glimpse the nape of his neck, that pale gap
exposed as if to the axe, revealing

silver wisps escaped from his surgeon's cap.
Bright lights set them gleaming, brightness a call,
like frail hands that haul me across the map

to this special scene, this sweet especial
rural scene: Ullswater in the foreground,
hills folding into the dark lake, a fall

of cataract, scattered flowers we found
beneath the golden grove of autumn trees
unleaving. And you, feet kicking through mounds

of leafmeal. On the grass our picnic tea
fussy with crisps, cake, unaware of how
this ends – curls sticky with ice cream, a sea

of brightness and the willows bending low
as though to catch you ... The cruellest loss,
they say, yet ... here you are. Which goes to show

echoes do linger, far beyond chaos,
murmurings that bloom in space to fashion
earth's sympathy, violets by a mossy

stone. The nurse said it was an illusion,
a chemical reaction in the brain,
said I'd been a gonner, I'd looked ashen,

seven minutes to get me back again.
I asked her if the surgeon had grey hair
but she just smiled, advised me to refrain

from going there. Through a window fresh air,
bird song, the planet breathing like a prayer.

Saying Goodbye

(for SC)

rain falls
trains run late
unwanted
the dog day dawns

crematorium
not a word to trip from the tongue
but mumble stumbling
on numbed lips

above its tall chimney
spirals loss
fragments of memory
cloud-bound

in the village hall we gather
to watch her pour tea
hug friends
insist nervously

Sarah's daughter
eerily here
in this no-man's-land
of disbelief

disturbing doppelgänger
red-haired haunting
from yesterday
when we too were young

Longing

Breath on the back of my neck,
fingertips that slip away,
footsteps behind me
fading the more I strain to hear,
felt like a shiver in the gut,
the gravitational pull of planets,
a gene lurking in strands of DNA
like a song bound to endless repeats.
I catch you in unsuspecting mirrors,
a ghost in peripheral vision,
the glance I cannot stop,
the *res mirabilis* promise of bliss.
Turning round is irresistible.
We are all Orpheus.

We are all Orpheus.
Turning round is irresistible,
the *res mirabilis* promise of bliss,
the glance I cannot stop.
A ghost in peripheral vision,
I catch you in unsuspecting mirrors
like a song bound to endless repeats,
a gene lurking in strands of DNA,
the gravitational pull of planets
felt like a shiver in the gut,
fading the more I strain to hear
footsteps behind me,
fingertips that slip away,
breath on the back of my neck.

On The Somme

They're just children
fighting at the front,
bayoneting each other with
biros. They've elbowed me aside
to reach the small, printed notice:
this many dead, that many wounded,
these few yards gained;
they bicker over worksheets,
scribble mind-numbing numbers
in eyebrow pencil, swap gum, compare lip gloss,
its red stain bubbling
from pursed mouths, strawberry-flavoured.

An order barks out:
  Tyson! Put that back!
  Right everyone, hunker down …
provoking a rat-a-tat of protest, mutinous, unthinkable,
  It's wet, Sir …
  Mud on my jeans …
  My mum said you can't make us …
and I, lurking at the back, long to silence the guns,

as they did, as they must have done.
Pictures come of flesh on wire,
guts spilling, while Billy scrambles
over the top and is gone

for two seconds,
till Mr Jones hauls him back
and cuffs him round the ear.
  We'll go over together, he says, *a united assault…*

on memories that haunt the air
just beyond hearing.
I find pieces of shrapnel,
fail to count the countless white crosses,
read, stare, weep silently behind Lisa's
shock of curly hair which hides earphones.
She is humming hard rock, smiling

as she clambers up and …

we are all dead –
the whole group,
the whole school, for that matter –
in the blink between word and madness.
That's what he said, Mr Jones,
  You'd all be dead by now.

Coffin Road

From east to west we bear them
over earth skinned to bone,
where peat banks leer round corners,
blackwater pools suck your feet,
iron sky looms
and life is squeezed from stone.

In long lament we bear them,
this last journey back
to where the gentle lie,
stumbling as we sing a space,
a place deep enough to cradle souls –
except for auld MacKay's
who woke up. We heard him groan,
bang the lid,
so we turned around
till next time.

There is no giving up.
Along the track, down the trail,
across the bitter hillsides
hanging sheep-littered, stone-wracked,
one last summit, crest the rise,
and just before we think resolve might fail –
a suddenness of colour
wild enough to stop the heart.

However many words we know for blue,
they are not enough
for what we see:
that blinding view
of waves rolling from shore to endless shore,
the breath of home and whispered grace,
sand whiter even than before,

green machair,
eyebright, heath orchid, red clover, thrift, heartsease.

Coffin Road is the local name for The Harris Walkway, Outer Hebrides. It is a rough mountain track along which, after the Highland Clearances, islanders would carry their dead, from the inhospitable rocks and peat bogs of the east to the Atlantic coast, where there was sufficient depth of soil to bury them.

When She Died

he tried digging a hole to plant
grief, next to geranium and begonia;
the soil, alluvium-rich, crumbled
through his fingers
like chocolate cake
baked by Ellen for tea on the lawn.
Across the grass, shadows cast
by deckchairs; comfortable shapes
with legs outstretched –
the possibility, as geo-phys suggests,
of archaeology.

He lifts turf
laid when they made the garden together.
Where spade cuts dirt, flashbacks
worm the surface: Ellen, bright in sparkly earrings;
three feet more and Ellen cycles by
refusing to wear a helmet.
Memories swarm his boot, vanish
down a crack, invite pursuit.
He jumps in to excavate, uncovers
Roman coins, pottery, her quirky smile,
tunnels far beneath the house, the street –

soon he will reach the beginning,
where garden sheds are trees
and bricks the sand of ancient seas
that lap the feet of dinosaurs.
He will wade through
swamp, descend barren rock,
dive the pyroclastic flow,
brave tongues of volcanic flame
that burn the air,
crawl on and on until he finds her
waiting for him there.

Elixir

They say
that household dust is mainly
human skin,
which means that
underneath this pile of clothes,
behind the golf bag and eighty-three
copies of Fisherman's Weekly,
at the back of the cupboard,
a million million particles
  of   you
    stir,
  then rise   and spin
like   fragile   stars,
    moments of used-to-be woken
  by a sweeping   brush
    to fill the room before
        drifting   down
      onto my eyes
  and   nose
and mouth
that gulps you in
starving
for a smile, a word,
one of your really bad jokes,
anything –
so hungry I devour
morsels, gobble atoms
deep inside
until I swell,
pregnant
with love's alchemy
that feeds on what we most desire
  (a kind of resurrection?)
  and I am overflowing.

Regeneration

I lay her carefully upon the kitchen table, reverently perhaps. Try not to hurt, imagining pain, discomfort, bones that might snap. She looks oddly taut and white, not as I remember her at all. With an old pair of scissors I cut through the autopsy stitches, science-sewn. I open her up. And as the flaps of skin ease apart, all that was tied down bursts forth: buds wink from eager twigs; saplings creak then twang into free air; roots snake around the table leg; leaves green from the foetid rest of what was once my Aunt Joan and rustle in time to the kitchen clock. Soon there'll be space for nesting birds; an owl or two, at dusk.

The incision line is ragged. Like someone took a rusty wood saw to her chest, leaving drifts of sawdust to cushion the aorta. Which is good, because she was always soft-hearted. Leaning forwards, I peer into the cavity, deep into its dark, primordial mystery. Where Leonardo mused and Darwin theorised, I sprinkle rooting compound. Now there'll be fertile soil for hedera, wild bluebells, primrose, anemone, celandine, lush ground cover for the Heath Fritillary. In the cool of afternoon, soft wings flutter past.

Brown eye meet mine and Joanie winks at me through a knothole in a tree trunk. The air fills with birdsong and I elbow my way through the undergrowth, shoving branches aside to reach the kettle. Time for tea.

The Call Of Home

Tell me when.
Monday morning, just as the sun is rising.

Heading for?
Rockall, Malin, Finisterre.

What draws you there?
Storm 10 veering west, poor, becoming moderate.

Because you miss?
Parsley, sage, the rolling road.

Who knows of your coming?
Birds of the air; Tom Pearce, Bill Brewer, Peter Gurney ...

Why me?
Oak, ash and greenwood tree.

What is it you seek?
Silver bells, cockleshells, fleece white as snow.

Can you care so?
My delight, in sunshine or in shadow.

And your new-found land?
Is not mine; when the bough breaks ...

What went wrong?
Summer's gone and all the flowers are dying.

Your needs?
A rabbit skin, a pocket full of rye.

To guide your footsteps?
Seven stars, six proud walkers.

I am waiting.
Like a candle in the window of a house.

Indigo Dreams Publishing Ltd
24, Forest Houses
Cookworthy Moor
Halwill
Beaworthy
Devon
EX21 5UU
www.indigodreams.co.uk